A MAN'S
WORSHIP
AND WITNESS

*A study of how
God's Kingdom
comes to and
through men*

Jack Hayford

THOMAS NELSON PUBLISHERS
Nashville • Atlanta • London • Vancouver

ISBN 0-7852-7797-8

Printed in the United States of America

1 2 3 4 5 6 7 - 01 00 99 98 97 96 95

*This message was originally brought at
The Church On The Way.*

*It has since been edited and revised
for publication by Pastor Hayford,
in partnership with Pastor Bob Anderson,
Director of Pastoral Relations.*

TABLE OF CONTENTS

Chapter One
Right to the Center!

A Street-Level Application

There's a central core of pivotal possibilities in every man. This "center of being" so foundational in each of us is interchangeably called our "heart" or "spirit." It's called our heart because (like our physical heart) it is central to our life and effective functioning; and (like our emotional "heart") this "core" determines our primary focus, interests, and affections in life. This "core" is also called our spirit because it's central to touching God—the Source of our life and Resource of power to live it. Our worshiping the Almighty God is the key to activating and revitalizing this "core." Our worship "connects" us with Him:

• Like a "landsat" uplinks to capture a picture and message from a satellite in space.

• Like an elevator built into the hub of a high-rise, allowing contact and interaction at every floor level.

• Like a ski lift takes us from the plain of the mundane to the peak of adventure.

I had just finished a workshop on worship, and Jack had been one of the men present. You'd like him—a tough-but-gentle, strong-but-quiet guy—a contractor in the roofing business and a committed disciple of Jesus Christ. He had been there as I'd outlined the principles of power in my message: *When a Man Worships.* Like so many of the hundreds of men I meet with monthly, Jack was getting hold of the fact that spirituality isn't mystical; that operating in continual touch with the Immortal, Invisible, Almighty God isn't a lapse into mindlessness or bizarre behavior.

We'd just looked at Abraham, who the Bible says "fathered" the way of faith for men like us, and among the power-principles we noted in Abraham's worship was the power of his footsteps. God told him, "Walk through the land I've promised you!" Abraham had done it because he believed his obedience was an act of worship, moving in to possess God's promised boundaries for his life. Jack's mind was gripped by this revelation in God's Word, reminding him that the worship of his heart was more than a meditative, devotional exercise—it was spiritually dynamic and impacting of a man's "outer" world as well as his inner thoughts. He was learning that as a man worships his Creator, his spirit—his inner being—is endowed with a "weight of glory." He saw how that "weight"—a pure vein of Heaven-born substance to his life, filling the core, or center of his being as he worships, is intended by God to be a means for pointedly dealing with practical daily issues and problems.

Jack and Julie had been having trouble

8

with their teenaged daughter, Cathy. A good kid had suddenly begun behaving strangely. A rebellion not present before was starting to stress the family's relationship with Cathy, and strained moments were crowding into a happy home.

Armed with this lesson on the power in the faith-filled footsteps of a worshiping man, Jack rose early the next morning before the family or neighbors were up and about. In the dim light of that predawn hour, he went outside and began to walk the property line bordering their home site. As he stood at each corner, he lifted his hands in praise to the Almighty, then strode forward with worship, doing two things:

• Declaring the might and glory of God, exalting His greatness, power, and love; and

• Calling on God's power to surround his home—to overrule any evil power seeking to penetrate the boundaries of his family's life.

Jack's worship-filled action was rewarded with incredible speed and precision.

Later that morning, right after Jack had left for work and Cathy for school, Julie, while washing the breakfast dishes, was impressed with a clear picture which came to her mind. She saw herself entering her daughter's room, opening a specific drawer, reaching to the back of the drawer under specific garments, and finding a small packet. She sensed God's presence prompting her and quickly dried her hands and did exactly what she had just "seen." As a result, she discovered a package of marijuana in that precise location, obviously hidden there by their daughter.

When Cathy arrived home from school, Jack and Julie lovingly, but pointedly, confronted her. Jack first described how God had moved him to walk in worship around their home, inviting God's power— "Thy Kingdom come!" Next, Julie related her experience at the kitchen sink, and her pursuant action. Then, laying the small packet before Cathy, they expressed their love for her and their desire to help—words that were instantly met with a teenager's tears and overflowing words of repentance. "Mom, Dad, I didn't really want this stuff. . .I don't know why I've been like I've been. . .but I know this is Jesus' way of stopping me. Thank you. . .Thank you. . . ." And amid more tear-filled eyes, a family was bonded closer than ever, and unknown, potentially devastating possibilities were averted.

It's just one example of the power of what I call "hardcore worship." If the core-like center of a man's being—his heart/his spirit—becomes filled with the solid gold of living praise, vital power will result. It's born through childlike humility in a man's worship before the Creator. It's the "praise with understanding" that brings the dimension of divine blessing into practical daily application. And it discovers and invites the power of God's Kingdom, over and above the efforts of the darkness to crowd out His glory-brightness from our homes or any part of our lives. Let's find out how we can each draw on this resource of power-through-worship.

Worship Defined

It's wonderful to hear the testimony of Jack's employing worship so effectively, but some people may be troubled by this "using" of worship. Aren't we supposed to worship God only for *His* sake, never for our *own*?

Of course, it's true that God Himself IS the object, the focus, and the centerpiece Personality of all worship—He Himself! But I believe He has made clear in His Word that He has more in mind and purpose through our worshiping Him than just Himself. He has *given* us His call to worship to release things both in us and through us as worshiping men. I contend that God instituted worship *for people*—not solely for *His* own enjoyment.

• I submit that worship is not intended by God for people to prove their own expertise in religious exercise, but that rather He gave us worship as a means for satisfying our hunger and thirst for Him.

• I propose that Sunday mornings were never designated as a weekly test to prove whether we love God or not, but that rather

He gave us His biblical call to worship together (Hebrews 10:25) to keep us in the mainstream of spiritual refreshing via worship, teaching, and fellowship.

• I contend that when worship focuses on "protecting God" from "unworthy" participants—disallowing participation by people who have not met some religious standard of desirability, sophistication, or compatibility—then its purpose is defeated. Such restrictive attitudes can never serve God's purpose as a means to bringing broken people into wholeness and fulfillment.

• I hold that worship is *for people*. You see, God did not first *receive* worship. He first *gave* it; creating man with this dynamic capacity, and it's very clear that God's mindset in "giving" worship as a potential exercise for mankind had man's best interests at heart. For example, the first gift given toward focusing worship was God's gift of the Sabbath (Genesis 2:3); a gift from God which Jesus made clear was *indeed* for the benefit (Mark 2:27) of mankind. Sabbath worship (including church life and fellowship in the New Testament) has been given for the restoration of the human soul, for the blessings which He releases to us in the context of our communion with and worship of God. And yet, to illustrate how quickly mankind can distort what God designs, the Pharisees wrenched the Sabbath into a legalistic ordeal that didn't bless anyone as God had intended, but only served to puff the pride of theological experts.

There have always been some who disagree that a key purpose of worship is to bless the worshiper. Such a concept has been viewed as a self-serving brand of "experience-oriented" spirituality. *Anthropocentric*, they would call it—which is a fancy, tongue-splitting way of saying, "centered in man."

"In worship," they would emphatically state, "*God* is blessed and God alone! How dare *we* presume to be beneficiaries of the act of worship which is, by its very definition, a consecration of devotion *heavenward to God!*" That sounds so holy. But listen:

I would certainly agree, and would resist any brand of pop-theology or worship practice if it is only configured to satisfy a man's quest for God *while at the same time* allowing him to continue pursuing his own indulgences. In this respect, I would heartily agree—God and His glory are the focus of our praise, and our obedience to Him is the evidence of our commitment to Him. I say, "Amen!" We should beware of any self-serving religious exercises which, though choreographed under the banner of "worship," transform no one and transcend nothing. Thus, the "man-centeredness" which others insist we avoid is indeed addressed. But, in settling that issue, let us not fall into the camp of anyone who would fear the benefits of worship—people being "blessed" or holiness becoming too "happy" a lifestyle. Let's be sure to take into account the numerous scriptures which promise worshipers "blessings," "fruitfulness," and "increase" if we pursue the Lord with all of our heart:

> *I will sing a new song to You, O God; on a harp of ten strings I will sing praises to You. . .Happy are the people who are in such a state; happy are the people whose God is the Lord!*
>
> *Psalm 144:9, 15*

> *. . . I have come that they may have life, and that they may have it more abundantly.* *John 10:10*

We need to remember that in saying "worship is *for man*" does not mean that worship is *to him.* All worship, however benefiting it is to us, is directed to the Lord—we've made that clear. Even so, some may be disturbed at the thought that from God's perspective, the gift of worship He's given to us, His beloved creatures, is intended to *enrich, fulfill, bless,* and *benefit* the worshiper.

I want to emphasize that this is true.

Always.

And worship benefits us a lot.

Consider these biblical truths:

• When we give, it shall be given unto us (Lk. 6:38).

• God, like any good parent, is blessed

when His children are blessed (Mt. 7:11).

• Repeatedly, God calls His creatures to worship in His presence so that He might release, redeem, renew and restore them (Ps. 17:15; Jer. 17:14).

• The Bible virtually blossoms with such beautiful affirmation: God intends that in worship His people would find joy, blessing, fulfillment and purpose (Ps. 9:14; Ps. 43:4; Isa. 61:3).

A Dramatic Illustration

One of the most dramatic pictures of this principle is manifest in the way God delivered Israel and brought them to be a people who would learn to truly worship Him. The broken yoke of their Egyptian taskmasters opened the way to a meeting at Mount Sinai where they not only received God's commandments—He also gave them the tabernacle worship as a means of walking into a *life* of worship, which would *lead* to a *land* of His fulfilling purpose for them. When God called them forth so that they might "serve Me" (i.e., worship Him), He wasn't relocating them from one form of slavery to another—from Egypt's bricks to Sinai's rituals. No! He was leading them to a life of blessing; to a life of discovering that if you worship the Living God, you'll receive His promised purpose for you, and by that worship and its attendant blessing, you'll become a witness to the world.

He delivered His people out from bondage

and into worship, for it was only through worship that Israel could come to fully know God's heart and nature. Further, only through worship would they begin to grasp the far-reaching purposes of the One who had promised "I will bring you up and bring you in . . . to a land flowing with milk and honey." And their experience is a graphic picture of what it means, through worship, to know the God of your destiny, who designs His people to be great and to have real purpose on this earth. Just as Abraham, the Father of Faith, journeyed from altar to altar, worshiping the Lord through his lifetime as he was led by God, so Israel, and so we are called. See what He said to Abraham:

> *I will make you a great nation; I will*
> *bless you and make your name great;*
> *and you shall be a blessing.*
> *Genesis 12:2*

Capture the significance of that statement! It applies to you and me, revealing God's purpose for and through all who worship Him. God's original and ongoing design in redemption is not only to bless us who worship Him, but also to bless *through* us. Our worship becomes the pivotal point at which God not only meets us to minister to us, but where He transforms us and blesses us so He can minister through us. Our Father's high design is to bless the world through a "nation" of worshipers—

people who will become witnesses unto His glory:

Arise, shine; for your light has come! And the glory of the Lord is risen upon you. For behold, the darkness shall cover the earth, and deep darkness the people; but the Lord will arise over you, and His glory will be seen upon you. The Gentiles shall come to your light, and kings to the brightness of your rising. Isaiah 60:1-3

But you are a chosen generation, a royal priesthood, a holy nation, His own special people, that you may proclaim the praises of Him who called you out of darkness into His marvelous light. 1 Peter 2:9

It is this understanding that will keep us motivated purely, sensibly, and openly in our worship. Our praise will never be a mere show of pretense in worship, as if we could somehow manipulate blessings from God. Our first and foremost reason to worship will be to fulfill our Lord's words:

Then one of the scribes came and . . . asked Him, "Which is the first commandment of all?" Jesus answered him, "The first of all the commandments is: 'Hear, O Israel, the Lord our God, the Lord is one. And you shall love the Lord your God with all your heart, with all your soul, with all your mind, and with all your strength.' This is the first commandment. And the second, like it, is this: 'You shall love your neighbor as yourself.' There is no other commandment greater than these."   Mark 12:28-31

See the direct relationship between *prioritizing* worship and *actualizing* our expression of God's love to those around us. Vital worship to God transforms the soul and brings a genuine concern for our "neighbor"—the world around us. From all these insights we distill these principles.

• Worship was and is our fulfillment of God's foremost *commandment*.
• Worship was and is the touchpoint of *relationship*—ours, both with God and with man.
• Worship was and is the entrypoint to finding and fulfilling God's intended *destiny* for one's life.
• Worship was and is the releasepoint of great *blessing to us*.
• Worship was and is the power-point by which we are transformed and empowered to become *witnesses* to the world around us.

This perspective on worship is abundantly evident in the New Testament as well. One of Jesus' most profound statements about worship included reference to an immoral woman (John 4:7-29). He was clearly welcoming her to turn away from her emptiness, to be filled with the love of the Living God, Who is seeking the worship of honest hearts—even broken ones like hers.

Paul in his epistle to the Romans calls us to present ourselves as people of worship so we can come to know the goodness, the desirability, and the perfection of God's purpose in our lives (ref. Romans 12:1, 2).

Such illustrations from Scripture clearly show that IF we worship Him in spirit and in truth, esteeming Him worthy of all praise, all the benefits of worship are inescapable! In other words, God is SEEKING genuine worshipers, and wherever He can find them, you can be sure He will bless them and accomplish His purposes through them. How, then, should we think about our worship as men who are learning this wisdom?

He Is Worthy!

Get your tongue ready. Here comes a real twister: *weorthscipe.* Any serious word study of "worship" will ultimately bring you to this archaic word. It's Old English, meaning "to ascribe worth, to pay homage, to reverence or to venerate." The common ground between weorthscipe's definition and the word "worship," is the concept of *worth.* When we connect the idea of *worth* with the action of *worship,* a few interesting questions arise.

• What value or *worth* are we ascribing to God in our worship?

• Is our worship *proportionate* to God's actual character and glory?

• Do our worshipful *expressions* of devotion transcend mere intellectual assessments of God, and do they involve *heartfelt affection* and *expressed love* for the Lord?

It would be wise to take inventory of our worship, to assess it in the light of Scripture. For example, let's take a lesson from the ultimate earthly expression of worship—Solomon's Temple. On the day it was completed, God's pleasure with all that had been done was abundantly evident:

And they brought up the ark of the Lord . . . King Solomon, and all the congregation (were) sacrificing sheep and oxen that could not be counted or numbered for multitude. Then the priests brought in the ark of the covenant of the Lord . . . And it came to pass, when the priests came out of the holy place, that the cloud filled the house of the Lord, so that the priests could not continue ministering because of the cloud; for the glory of the Lord filled the house of the Lord.

1 Kings 8:4-6,10-11

Don't miss the significance of this visitation of God's glory responding to a man's worship. What brought it about?

First, *immeasurable worth* was being ascribed to the Lord through the glorious Temple worship. No expense had been spared. It has been estimated that the entire project of Solomon's Temple cost approximately $4 trillion! Of course, Solomon was not confused by thinking that the shimmer of layers of gold and precious gems in the Temple WAS God's glory. On the contrary, he was awestruck with his God:

> *But will God indeed dwell on the earth? Behold, heaven and the heaven of heavens cannot contain You. How much less this temple which I have built!*
> *1 Kings 8:27*

Solomon recognized the incomprehensibility of the Almighty. He knew that God transcended any religious enterprise of man—that God could not be captured or contained inside a building or a method. But he also knew that God's presence would dwell richly wherever worthy worship was raised to His glory. In short, my brother, you and I can build a house of worship any place we decide, and it doesn't cost $4 trillion, $4 million, $4 thousand, or even 4 cents: it costs much more. A man's worship costs the full commitment of his heart—the core of his life and affection—unto God.

A Summary of Insights
God's visitation at the site of Solomon's Temple gives us a fivefold insight to the main

components of worship—a man's worship which makes a place for God's glory to manifest. These components include:

1. A *physical expression* of God's worth. This was evidenced in the very fact of His building the Temple. This represents a man's "making room" for the Lord to dwell where he is (1 Kings 6:1-38). This is the starting place: Make a place in your daily life, or build a place in any circumstance you face—give God "room" to work there.

2. A *conceptual grasp* of God's worth was expressed in Solomon's articulate, insightful prayer of dedication, extolling God's grandeur and majesty (1 Kings 8:22-53). When you worship, remember brother, we're worshiping an awesome God, Who is greater and grander than we can possibly imagine. Faith rises in such an atmosphere of worship and praise.

3. A *financial proclamation* of God's worth was declared by the huge investment made in the Temple, all of which came from free-will offerings presented by worshipers of the Lord (1 Kings 7:13-51). Never minimize the righteous wisdom of bringing tithes and offerings as you worship. We can't buy God's blessings, but disobedience in worship can prevent them.

4. A *spiritual statement* of worth was made by the countless sacrifices offered that day during the celebration of the Temple's dedication (1 Kings 8:62-66). Always remember that the heartbeat of all

living worship pulsates with the awareness that the Blood of the Lamb is (a) the means of our access to God's throne in worship, (b) the power which cleanses us as priestly men for worship, and (c) the promise of victory which overthrows the enemy as we worship.

5. A *divine visitation* resulted—the consequence of a man's worship opened the way for the entrance of God's glory and power, right there and right then (1 Kings 8:1-11). This same prospect is available today as you and I worship the Lord: He's ready to visit with transforming glory, to change our natures and to change our circumstance, right here—right now!

This is important enough for us to review and apply all these things again. As worshiping men, let's lay hold of the significance of each facet of the above.

Physical expression. Simply put, God's man gave God room. It was only a building—a Temple—but it symbolizes how each one of us may daily prepare a chamber of worship in our hearts—make room. Obviously, "to make room" will often require the elimination of clutter and obstructions. Even with the most sincere believer, worldly debris and carnal distractions can gradually crowd the heart. Suddenly, without ever having realized the quantity of these things, we find ourselves encumbered by the stuff of this world—"stuff" which seeks to suffocate the praises of God. Whether it's anxieties, sin, distractions—whatever would steal from God

23

His rightful place on the throne of our hearts—such obstructions are rightfully called "idols."

> *Son of man, these men have set up their idols in their hearts, and put before them that which causes them to stumble into iniquity. Should I let Myself be inquired of at all by them? Therefore speak to them, and say to them, "Thus says the Lord God: 'Everyone of the house of Israel who sets up his idols in his heart, and puts before him what causes him to stumble into iniquity, and then comes to the prophet, I the Lord will answer him who comes, according to the multitude of his idols, that I may seize the house of Israel by their heart, because they are all estranged from Me by their idols.'"*   *Ezekiel 14:3-5*

Conceptual grasp. In J.B. Phillips' classic book, *Is Your God Too Small?*, he challenges the reader to come to grips with how often and how severely we each tend to minimize God in our own thinking. It happens naturally because our finite minds so easily tend toward thinking of God in human terms. Further, this happens frequently because the Adversary of our souls will constantly seek to undermine our faith by blurring our vision of the greatness of our God. But worship is the perfect opportunity to clear and to enlarge our vision, to let the Holy Spirit expand our perceptions, and to refresh our exposure to the Living God. David was diligent to remind himself Who his God was and how worthy He was of his continual trust.

When I consider Your heavens, the work of Your fingers, the moon and the stars, which You have ordained, what is man that You are mindful of him, and the son of man that You visit him?

Psalm 8:3-4

I will meditate on the glorious splendor of Your majesty, and on Your wondrous works.   *Psalm 145:5*

Financial proclamation. Our tithes and offerings affirm that God is worthy of our material sacrifice. When we give, we are saying in essence, "Lord, all that I have is from You to begin with. I trust You, and I freely and obediently give—not only because You command it, but because You are faithful and I know You will provide for all of my needs!" Simple obedience in this area of giving stems from God's Word, and it's rich with promise.

"Bring all the tithes into the storehouse, that there may be food in My house, and prove Me now in this," says the Lord of hosts, "If I will not open for you the windows of heaven and pour out for

25

*you such blessing that there will not
be room enough to receive it."*
Malachi 3:10

Spiritual statement. Foremost, our
worship magnifies the covenant of
Calvary—the Blood of the Lamb. But
Solomon's sacrifices, according to the Old
Testament covenant anticipating Calvary,
are instructive in additional ways. Look at
the way he made sacrifices of innumerable
offerings.

It may seem surprising that Scripture
describes praise and worship as a "sacrifice." As men at worship, exactly what are
we sacrificing, anyway? What are we losing?

Primarily, our "flesh." Just as animals'
flesh was consumed on the altar with
Solomon's offering of bulls and lambs, so
our carnality ("flesh") may be consumed
by the fire of God's Presence as we worship.
Pride dies. Sophistication fades. Self-
sufficiency is abandoned as we acknowl-
edge our utter dependence upon God
through worship and extol His worthiness
to receive our thanksgiving and praise.

*Therefore by Him let us continually
offer the sacrifice of praise to God, that
is, the fruit of our lips, giving thanks to
His name . . . for with such sacrifices
God is well pleased.*
Hebrews 13:15, 16

Worthy worship ascribes all these things to the glory of the Lord. The result will always be a **Divine visitation**. We'll be changed and our circumstances, however restrictive, will be transcended by God's power. Those are the reasons He's "given" us worship; the reasons He's delivered us from our own "Egyptian" slavery. He's called us to be men of worship, but with the heart-qualities of a child. God is well pleased with such a spirit, for thereby the "core" of your being is becoming filled with the solid gold of His character and understanding. Such a childlikeness of this "hardcore worship" is not child*ish*. But it's that order of manly worship and tender-hearted trust seen in that no-nonsense roofing contractor, Jack. Though equipped with a workman's hands of granite, this man chose to be blessed with a heart as tender as a child's toward God; who, walking in the predawn hours with upraised arms around his property in worshipful dependence upon God, discovered the pathway for his family's deliverance.

Whatever our need,
    whomever we're concerned for,
        whatever we face—

Let's be men of worship like that.

TALK ABOUT IT! Chapter questions to discuss with a friend.

1. Have you ever had an experience similar to Jack's—where you felt the Lord called you to "walk the borders" of your home or apartment in prayer and worship? Share the results of your experience.

2. Do you think this is something men should do on a regular basis as priests of their homes? Decide when you will do this again, or for the first time, and find another brother to be accountable to regarding your commitment.

3. Do you still feel reservation about physical worship (raising hands, etc.)? Discuss your feelings about this with a brother.

Chapter Two
Your Body—His Temple

Do you ever feel like a spiritual "toad"?

That's the way I've often described my perception of myself on more occasions than I care to number. Even though I *know* it's right to worship, and even though I *love* the Lord with all my heart, I can feel as devoid of spirituality as a brass doorknob, as passionate for action as a tree sloth—that's what I mean when I describe my feelings as being on the order of a "toad."

Perhaps nothing challenges a man's worship more than coming to terms with the human inclination toward passivity. Presuming the barricades of pride have been overcome, and a child-like willingness to worship secured in my soul, any number of things can slow my readiness to worship like Jesus said.

And you shall love the Lord your God with all your heart, with all your soul, with all your mind, and with all your strength.　　　*Mark 12:30*

This text, summoning a man's worship of the Most High God with his total being—spirit, soul (mind, emotions, and will), and body, is matched with a similar summons from the lips of Paul:

> *I beseech you therefore, brethren, by the mercies of God, that you present your bodies a living sacrifice, holy, acceptable to God, which is your reasonable service. And do not be conformed to this world, but be transformed by the renewing of your mind, that you may prove what is that good and acceptable and perfect will of God.*
> *Romans 12:1, 2*

These verses are precious commands from God's Word, inciting us to worship expressively and tenaciously. But how often have "toadlike" feelings of inadequacy, weariness, guilt, or other human obstacles of mind or emotion hindered you? Private devotional times and public congregational meetings are equally blocked by such feelings. So, to become a man of worship, I've got to find the pathway to become dynamically equipped to worship God with an honesty toward my own feelings, but a willingness to exceed them by actions of my will and understanding.

Time and again, the psalms of David—certainly a man who learned the power of worship—declare "I WILL praise the Lord!" It's no secret that with many of the events in David's life, he was likely to often not "feel" much like worshiping. Alternately being chased by Saul—running for his life;

betrayed by his son—and running for his life again; desperately trapped at the hands of enemies; guilty of miserable failure as a victim of his own sin—such episodes hardly seem conducive to worshipful praise toward God. Yet David, as a man who knew the essence of adversity year after year, still continued praising God through it all.

It's a decision a man makes. So when the "spiritual toad" feelings beset us, whether due to weariness, discouragement, or failure, let's learn from David's example. The power of God's Word reporting David's overcoming praise can birth or renew a fortitude in us. Say with me, "I don't need to *feel* spiritual! I *will* to praise Your Name, O God!"

Join me as a partner in discovering what the Holy Spirit can do when such a posture of persistency in praise is taken. The Spirit of God will move into the moment, once you and I commit to praise irrespective of our feelings. He'll never view that action as mechanical or self-induced. He sees it for what it is—a will to exalt Jesus. . .a will to praise the Father. . .a will to live on the grounds of the Word notwithstanding circumstance or feelings. The Spirit of the Lord doesn't regard such assertiveness as hypocritical, as though requiring your feelings to bow before your will was somehow insincere because insufficient emotions were present. He can handle the fact that you're worshiping by reason of a determination to

31

praise, and that you're not a man dependent upon "warm fuzzy feelings." In fact, God is possibly *more* blessed by such a "sacrifice of praise," coming from a man's sheer gut-determination, rather than by occasional praises that might arise "whenever I feel like it"!

Here are three key points we can apply to our personal times of worship that will help us praise the Lord more expressively and more meaningfully.

1. *Personalize your praise.*

To begin, it's certainly appropriate to bring high praise to God for His great wonders, His manifold graces of kindness, His mightiness in creation, the beauty of His attributes, etc. That's "personal" in terms of thinking on *His* personal nature and works. Further, there's no higher purpose in praise and worship than to magnify the Savior, to express thanksgiving for His death on the Cross, His saving grace shown to you, and for His goodness in walking with you day to day. These are personal reasons for praise that focus on Jesus Himself. And the most devout Christian will never fully grasp the immensity of these concepts.

However, there are other dimensions of personalizing your praise, and they can be tremendously transforming to our attitudes when we come in worship. Bring your praise "on home!" Whatever the setting, praise Him for where you live; praise Him for the things He has been doing in your life; express praise to God for your family members; and how about your job? Whether good things or bad things have been happening in your career, praise Him! The power of praise will begin to tower above the worst things you face and will pour a shower of added glory around the best things:

In everything give thanks; for this is the will of God in Christ Jesus for you.
1 Thess. 5:18

Every good gift and every perfect gift is from above, and comes down from the Father of lights . . . *James 1:17*

Become a person given to *much* praise. Our absolute insurance against ever developing a bitter or perverse spirit, is for you and me as men of worship to be ever-thankful to God. A spirit of gratitude is heart-touched by even life's smallest blessings, and I remember being introduced to this grateful spirit by my Dad.

Indelible to my memory was one time, standing beside my father at a water fountain as he was drinking a glass of cold water. We'd both been working—I was giving it my teenaged best, while he was carrying the larger part of the load the task involved. As he finished, without pretended piety or any religious intonation, I heard him simply say, "Thank You, Lord, for this water." It was nothing loud or prolonged—he simply spoke the words. He noticed I was watching him closely at the moment, and turning to me, he said, "Son, I always thank the Lord for everything— including each glass of water. Not just on hot days in the middle of a job, but *every* time I take a drink." I don't know if it was because of the fact my father was a diabetic and thereby uniquely dependent upon the delicate chemical balance in his body, but somehow, some way, the Holy Spirit had touched a nerve of gratitude in him which touched my heart with under-standing: there's nothing too small for which to praise the Lord.

2. *Verbalize your praise.*

In some of my church background, I grew up in a spiritual environment where deep reverence was expected to be ex-pressed by one's silently bowing before God—and that's all. I learned the posture: eyes squeezed shut, hands folded, lips pursed silently in prayer. And I hasten to say, that such supposed requirements for the show of reverence certainly cannot be said to be "a bad thing." But frankly, it's worth asking the question, "How condu-cive is such silence to the expression of warmth and relationship?"

For example, if I come home from work and walk into the kitchen where my wife is cooking dinner, don't you imagine she'd be puzzled to see me stop, shut my eyes, bow my head, and with hands folded, expect her to "sense" I was bringing a loving greeting of my happiness to be with her and my gratitude for her care for home and family, not to mention her preparation of dinner? Of course, every couple has experienced moments of tender silence, simply sitting together, but love is essentially expressive and my dear lady, Anna, likes to hear me say, "I love you, honey."

Sure, I know that such a parallel of a husband-wife relationship with a worshiper coming before God may be an imperfect analogy. But it's not far off.

We were each created with a mouth, lips, and a tongue. We were given bodies to express and extend our communication. Could it be that God has no interest in their employment when we "commune" with Him? Would the Lord who formed our lips, tongue, and ears prefer our silence when we stand before Him?

Telling my wife about my love not only affirms her, it reinforces and deepens *my love* for her. Verbal confession is strong stuff.

So as you stand, kneel, or sit before the Lord, TELL Him your praise. SPEAK your worship! SING your exaltations! ARTICU-LATE your deepest feelings and thoughts. This isn't simply "making noise," but it's voicing biblical expressions:

My heart is steadfast, O God, my heart is steadfast; I will sing and give praise...

35

I will praise You, O Lord, among the peoples; I will sing to You among the nations. . . In the midst of the congregation, I will praise You.

Psalm 57:7, 9; 22:22

I assure you, brother, VERBALIZING worship can become like a drill bit that will plummet deeper into your being, tapping the possibilities of a new oil of anointing upon your life and the discovering of new riches of intimacy with your Creator.

3. *Mobilize your body.*

Telling my wife that I love her is much better than just thinking it. And better yet is to accompany my words of love with a tangible expression of it with a hug or a kiss. Likewise, engaging the emotions in worship means engaging my body in worship, too.

There are many ways to employ one's body in worship. But before we explore some of them, perhaps we need to address the matter of reserve along these lines. Unfortunately, even though the Bible is *very* pointed in its call to *physical* worship, some negate its importance. I appreciate the fears and the reserve which a few instances of fanaticism may have imposed on thoughtful worshipers. But to become biblical in the physical aspect of our worship is not a sectarian exercise, and a balanced view of physical worship can soon be seen as a logical, natural expression of our relationship with God. This is an added dimension of worship that the Holy Spirit will help us grow into. You don't want to be a fanatic and neither do I, but we can both trust the Holy Spirit. He is artfully gracious—always!—and can grow us into these expressions of worship without turning either of us into writhing weirdos.

Worship With Rededicated Bodies

Look closely with me at the fact the Lord sees your body and mine as a temple of His dwelling and as a literal, physical place not only for His occupancy, but as a center of His being magnified—glorified by what we do with our bodies as well as our spirits.

Or do you not know that your body is the temple of the Holy Spirit who is in you, whom you have from God, and you are not your own? For you were bought at a price; therefore glorify God in your body and in your spirit, which are God's.
1 Corinthians 6:19-20

Now let us reason together a moment. If *our **love** for the Lord is to flow from **all** of our entire being and strength*, should we be surprised that Scripture also directs our ***worship*** of the Lord to be expressed with **all** *of our being*—including our bodies? Biblical worship is powerful, not only because it involves every facet of our being, but also because it gloriously transforms us. Whatever part of ourselves or our lives we invest in worship becomes an instrument of ministry, receiving empowerment for becoming God's witnesses.

We've already made clear we're to worship the Lord with our minds, with pure emotions, with our spirits, and our bodies. But let's review in detail the Bible's "anatomy of worship," for it unsurprisingly brings us to the completion of a "grand tour" of our entire being at worship—mind, heart, soul, feelings. . .and body. Look with me at this catalog of scriptural directives which, text by text, call your and my whole physical being to respond in magnifying the Lord.

Knees

Few of us are unaware of the appropriateness of kneeling in prayer, praise, and worship to God, but how many understand the dynamic significance of the bowed knee? It's the symbol of submission—the spiritual indicator that I am yielding to the mastery of the Master. The Centurion who came to Jesus in Luke 7 recognized that a man *submitted* to authority becomes a man *endowed* with authority. **Knees** bowed in worship will become knees powerful in prayer. Interceding knees bring crowns of spiritual power upon the heads of those who pray—and worship paves the way.

Therefore humble yourselves under the mighty hand of God, that He may exalt you in due time.   1 Peter 5:6

*Therefore God also has highly exalted Him and given Him the name which is above every name, that at the name of Jesus every **knee** should bow, of those in heaven, and of those on earth, and of those under the earth.*
Philippians 2:9-10

Heads

As surely as it may be bowed in appropriate humility, the **head** of a redeemed man ought also to be lifted upward in praise. It's the posture of confidence. The head that is lifted up in worship becomes emboldened as it realizes it has been graced with authority. When the Lord lifts my head as I worship Him, I'll find new assurance to serve confidently in love, instead of exercising a pseudo authority that's "heady" in the human sense—brash, loud, pushy, inclined to intimidate others, or given to high-sounding religiousness.

*But You, O Lord, are a shield for me, my glory and the One who lifts up my **head**.   Psalm 3:3*

*Let us therefore come **boldly** to the throne of grace, that we may obtain mercy and find grace to help in time of need.   Hebrews 4:16*

Hands

Aside from the voice lifted in song or verbal praise, upraised **hands** are the most common physical expression of worship mentioned in the Bible. The Hebrew word for thanksgiving includes in its definition "the extension of the hands as with a choir of worshipers." The most natural expression any of us show when either grateful or rejoiced in our hearts is to extend our hands in appreciation or triumph. Further, hands lifted up to God in praise become hands that are willing to serve, and hands that are ready to touch with the healing power of Jesus.

*Therefore, I desire that the men pray everywhere, lifting up holy **hands**, without wrath and doubting.*
1 Timothy 2:8

*Thus I will bless You while I live; I will lift up my **hands** in Your name.*
Psalm 63:4

While there is not time to elaborate the biblical doctrine of "the laying on of hands" (see Hebrews 6:2), one thing is certain: worshiping hands can become direct extensions of Jesus' touch on this earth, and therein is great power.

*His brightness was like the light; He had rays flashing from His **hand**, and there His power was hidden.*
Habakkuk 3:4

Lips

Verbal praise is not simply an exercise of the mouth, tongue, and lips for the immediate moment alone. All worship expressions are not only to magnify the Lord, but to give place to His transforming work in you and me. If my lips are speaking from my heart, two things will happen: (1) My speech mechanisms will, through this act of dedication, be refined and equipped for better speaking to those around me in the spirit of God's love and truth; (2) My open declaration will have a way of sealing my commitments, breaking down doubt and neutralizing hypocrisy and the fear of man. The **mouth** that is opened with praise will be empowered by the Holy Spirit to declare God's Word to others with **lips** that speak the truth in love.

*O Lord, open my **lips**, and my mouth shall show forth Your praise.*
                              Psalm 51:15

*Because Your lovingkindness is better than life, my **lips** shall praise You.*
                              Psalm 63:3

*My **lips** shall greatly rejoice when I sing to You, and my soul, which You have redeemed.   Psalm 71:23*

Tongue

In league with my lips, the **tongue** tuned to the truth of worship will never fall prey to the duplicity of which James spoke:

41

*. . .The **tongue** is a little member and boasts great things. See how great a forest a little fire kindles! And the tongue is a fire, a world of iniquity. The tongue is so set among our members that it defiles the whole body, and sets on fire the course of nature; and it is set on fire by hell. For every kind of beast . . .has been tamed by mankind. But no man can tame the tongue. It is an unruly evil, full of deadly poison.*
James 3:5-8

But there is a means of transforming the tongue through worship. The tongue that extols the Most High will learn how to build up others, just as surely as it has learned to magnify God.

*There is one who speaks like the piercings of a sword, but the **tongue** of the wise promotes health.*
Proverbs 12:18

*And my **tongue** shall speak of Your righteousness and of Your praise all the day long.*   *Psalm 35:28*

*My heart is overflowing with a good theme; I recite my composition concerning the King; my **tongue** is the pen of a ready writer.*   *Psalm 45:1*

Deliver me from the guilt of bloodshed,
O God, the God of my salvation, and my
tongue *shall sing aloud of Your righ-*
teousness. *Psalm 51:14*

Eyes

Jesus spoke of the eye of the heart or the soul—saying "the lamp of the body is the eye" (Matthew 6:22; Luke 11:34). At worship, the inner eye of the heart may be enlightened. Paul prayed for the Ephesians that "the eyes of your heart may see the Father's hopes for you" (Ephesians 1:17-18, author's paraphrase). There is no question that something transforming happens to the vision of a man at worship. Isaiah said, "I saw the Lord high and lifted up," and it changed the direction of his life from impurity to impassioned service for God (Isaiah 6:1-9). **Eyes** that behold the Lord transform the heart, and they become eyes that can see the lost, that perceive the pain of the broken, and envision ways to serve the needs of others.

Is it not to share your bread with the
hungry, and that you bring to your
house the poor who are cast out; when
*you **see** the naked, that you cover him,*
and not hide yourself from your own
flesh? *Isaiah 58:7*

*My **eyes** are ever toward the Lord, for*
He shall pluck my feet out of the net.
Psalm 25:15

*I will lift up my **eyes** to the hills—from whence comes my help?*

Psalm 121:1

*Unto You I lift up my **eyes**, O You who dwell in the heavens.*

Psalm 123:1

Feet

The worshiping man is called to stand in the Presence of the Lord. Psalm 134:1 speaks of those "who stand by night in the house of the Lord" at worship before His throne. To stand is to give full attention; to stand is to realize you've been welcomed. To stand is the opposite of a cowering, groveling stance. While kneeling indicates reverence, standing reflects understood acceptance and a readiness to be commissioned. Ephesians 6:10-18 repeatedly instructs the believer to "stand" that we may be equipped for victorious battle against our adversary. Our **feet**, then, represent our learning to take a stance by which we magnify the Lord while at praise, and commit to walk in obedience to follow pathways of peace and carry the Gospel to others.

*I have restrained my **feet** from every evil way, that I may keep Your word.*
Psalm 119:101

*How beautiful upon the mountains are the **feet** of him who brings good news,* *who proclaims peace, who brings glad tidings of good things, who proclaims salvation, who says to Zion, "Your God reigns!"* Isaiah 52:7

*If you turn away your **foot** from the Sabbath, from doing your pleasure on My holy day . . . and shall honor Him, not doing your own ways, nor finding your own pleasure, nor speaking your own words, then you shall delight yourself in the Lord . . .* Isaiah 58:13-14

*You have turned for me my mourning into **dancing**; You have put off my sackcloth and clothed me with gladness.* Psalm 30:11

Come with me into His presence, Sir. Come with me often. Let's meet at His throne as men who worship and as men who offer complete worship.

With every aspect of our lives.

With every part of our bodies.

With the entirety of our whole being.

Bless the Lord, O my soul; And all that is within me bless His holy name! Psalm 103:1

**TALK ABOUT IT! Chapter questions
to discuss with a friend.**

1. Discuss the reasons why worship
can help you to overcome those "spiritual-
toad" feelings. Share some experiences
with a brother wherein you overcame a
heavy or oppressive spiritual climate
through worship.

2. Discuss the difference between *willing* to praise the Lord and *feeling* like
praising the Lord. Do you feel hypocritical
at times when you worship the Lord without the exuberance that others appear to be
experiencing? How does this relate to your
understanding of a "sacrifice of praise"?

3. Here's an interesting experiment:
employ different physical posturings during your prayer times this month: kneeling,
standing, walking, laying prostrate; head
bowed, head lifted; hands upraised; etc.
and speak your praise *aloud* to the Lord.
Note the effects these various styles had on
your worship experience. You may be
surprised at the results of this experiment!

Chapter Three
Going Against the Grain

The *power* of biblical worship
    is explosive;
The *benefits* of worship
    are all-encompassing;
The *purpose* of worship
    is eternally profound; and thus,
The *opposition* to worship
    by the world-mind is fierce.

Simply put: hell's forces don't want you to be a worshiping man because they don't want you to become a dynamic witness for God.

> *We know that we are of God, and the whole world lies under the sway of the wicked one.* 1 John 5:19

And the influence of hell's dark powers on all our minds is often more pronounced than we'd like to think. World-mindedness tends to taint our worship as well.

> *And do not be conformed to this world, but be transformed by the renewing of your mind. . .* Romans 12:2

The "sway of the wicked one," mentioned above, denotes the ceaseless efforts of hell-ish forces to suppress the advancement of God's Kingdom any way they can. As a result, the world is a hostile environment for people committed to worshiping the Living God in "truth and in spirit." Dynamic worship "goes against the grain" of this world's sway. Therefore, the dimensions of worship to which God has called men are—by their very nature—confrontive.

The attacks may be head-on: doubt sown in your mind; or criticism or anger against your worship patterns. Or, they may be subtle: a temptation to a cool reserve, a hesitation toward expressiveness, or a caution in commitment. But they'll be there—count on it. If hell's forces can't utterly silence the worship of God's people, they will try to pollute, weaken, or cripple its articulate expression. The spirit of the world has made these demands concerning worship:

• If you believe in God, then have *a quiet moment.*

(That's dignified.)

• If you believe in God, express it in *a theological thought.*

(That's respectable.)

• If you believe in God, *do a good deed* to display your worthiness.

(That's laudatory.)

. . . But *whatever* you do, DON'T be demonstrative in worshiping God! Don't act as if you believe the Creator of the Universe is capable of personally enjoying and welcoming your *audible* praise! Don't dare express before God even a fraction of the *physical* enthusiasm, vigor and zeal that you do at a football game! After all, one activity is recreational and enjoyable, while the other is . . . well . . . religious!

So says the world. And that's the kind of thing it has always said. Listen to the voice of your world speaking against worship through the following historical incidents. These true stories all have one common denominator: the world will resist a man's physical expression of worship to God. The world doesn't care if you have silent meditation or cerebral affirmations about God—just as long as the physical, visible, audible realm isn't overtly penetrated. It's because the world insists on preserving its own comfort zones.

Cain's Assault Against Abel

Soiled hands placed the vegetables in a tidy arrangement on the rock altar. Cain felt proud of his display. His brother, Abel, had begun assembling his own offering hours ago and still wasn't done.

Cain was.

All Cain did was walk to his garden and pull up the fine specimens out of the ground. They had grown all by themselves. And the garden was close by. It all seemed so easy.

A smug smile curled Cain's lips. His brother—still searching out in the fields for an offering—was laboring for nothing, Cain mused. He looked again upon his grand, colorful altar. There it was.

Vegetables.

On the altar.

Easy.

This being one of his first offerings, Cain wondered what exactly was to happen next. Pondering this, he sat on a nearby stone and waited. He looked over at his brother's altar just as Abel came through the bushes carrying several ewe lambs. It wasn't long before the lambs were mounted on Abel's altar and slain.

Cain noticed that Abel's altar was smaller than his. Good.

Having sacrificed the animals on the altar, Abel walked several paces back and knelt in prayer. Cain felt uneasy. He hadn't done that. But he comforted himself by observing that Abel's altar was blood-stained and dirty, while his was neat, tidy and colorful: orange and red and yellow and green and—just then: Whoosh! Brilliant flames from out of nowhere—from another realm—licked up all of Abel's sacrifice! All of it! Cain jumped to his feet. A few ashes drifted in the breeze. The colorful harvest on Cain's altar remained defiantly the same—unchanged. Nothing happened to his.

Cain stormed off, angered and pouting. And it was later, as his tormented mind seethed with hatred and jealousy, that the Lord met him near a tall palm tree: "Why are you angry? And why has your countenance fallen? If you do well, will you not be accepted? And if you do not do well, sin lies at the door. And its desire is for you, but you should rule over it" (Genesis 4:6, 7).

Shortly, Cain's competitive jealousy grew to such intolerable levels that he rose in fury to kill his brother, Abel. And thus, the record teaches us: the first murder was born in the heart of a man who resisted God's ways of worship. The first victim of violence was a man who worshiped God physically, openly, and freely.

Conclusion: the world will violently persecute those who worship the Lord in childlike obedience, even while they themselves exalt their own pretense of religious piety.

From that point in history, open worship of the Most High God has always been challenged and scorned.

• Israel's physical expression of worship through the rite of circumcision—an act of obedience which cut human flesh in the process of identifying with the God of Abraham—was mocked by pagan societies. Circumcision would never cut the world's flesh. But besides refusing the blade themselves, in anger the ancient society scorned those who did circumcise; those whose commitment was so physically expressed, they openly declared their intimate commitment to the true God. Exodus 4:24, 26 demonstrates this world-mind rejection. The anger of Moses' Midianite wife is the evidence of the stance the world held toward circumcision; a reflection of the world's mindset toward those who commit themselves to overtly express their praise and commitment to the Lord.

• Moses begged Pharoah to let God's people go to worship in the wilderness. Although this would not harm the Egyptians in any way, still witnessing the consecration of the Jews to the true God chaffed at heathen flesh. Pharoah could not stand to allow such devotion go unbridled, free from imprisonment—even though the Egyptians were beginning to feel threatened by the great multitude of the Jewish nation within their borders. Pharoah would risk it to punish true spirituality.

• Daniel and his friends revealed an impressive devotion to the Lord, at the same time as they were serving high political offices in a secular kingdom. The price was a death sentence. Yet on two occasions they refused to discontinue worshiping the Lord even though immutable decrees had been contrived by jealous men seeking to unseat them. The famous lion's den and fiery furnace stories (Daniel 3, 6) demonstrate the world's resistance to men who worship God. But they also reveal how the constancy of these men occasioned their dramatic witness of God's saving power to a heathen nation. And it was all by worship!

Perhaps one of the most remarkable case studies of a man's manliness being challenged because of his commitment to praise God openly and joyously, is wrapped in the episode of King David's being confronted by his wife, Michal.

Michal's Mockery

It was a balmy day and Michal was home—irritated again at David's preoccupation with the Ark of the Covenant. He seemed more interested in that wooden box than anything else—constantly talking about his desire for the Presence of God, which, he claimed, resided wherever that box was. His spiritual interests rankled her. After all, it was a triumphant warrior in battle she had married, not a worshiper of an invisible God. And then she heard it. At first, it was the sound of trumpets, and then as it drew nearer, Michal thought she heard yelling, or was it singing?

And there was clapping outside, too!

She hurried to the window and, looking out, saw the large crowd of people advancing toward the city. And then she saw the Ark of God, which she knew David was bent on bringing to Jerusalem to be housed in the special tabernacle he had built for it.

She had to admit, the procession was an interesting sight, but certainly not of any great importance to anybody who knew anything about anything. At least, that was Michal's assessment.

Her gaze had just begun to leave the window, but her attention sprang back instantly—something had caught her eye. She suddenly stiffened, a mixture of amazement, anger, and embarrassment sending surges of adrenaline into her whole system. Her face reddened.

It couldn't be!   But it *was*!!

Her husband—this is impossible!!—the king, dancing before the Ark. And look—look what he's wearing!   Her emotions churned as she spoke a curse under her breath, looking at David who had shed his regal garments and who was now wearing only a light linen ephod—a humble priestly smock.   Michal's wrath wrenched her lips tight.   Her hand trembled as she held back the window lace, then—almost tearing the covering from off the window as she slapped the curtain closed, she stormed off to the inner chamber, slamming the door behind her.

It was later that evening when David, having completed his worshipful placement of the Ark in the Jerusalem Tabernacle, entered his home. He was instantly greeted by Michal's enraged countenance and sneering accusation:

> *. . . How glorious was the king of Israel today, uncovering himself today in the eyes of the maids of his servants, as one of the base fellows shamelessly uncovers himself!*   2 Samuel 6:20

David's partial disrobing before all his subjects, as he stripped his royal outer garment to allow freedom for dancing his praise to the Lord God of Israel was, in her opinion, inexcusable. However, David had hardly been guilty of stark nudity or an obscene display that day. He had only danced in joyous praise to God. He had been "leaping and whirling before the Lord." The biblical record says that as she watched him, "she despised him in her heart."

2 Samuel 6 records David's response to Michal's confrontation, not only contextualizing the whole episode with spiritual sensitivity, but describing the unique childlikeness of David's heart toward God:

(My dancing) was before the Lord, who chose me instead of your father and all his house, to appoint me ruler over the people of the Lord, over Israel. Therefore I will play music before the Lord, and I will be even more undignified than this, and will be humble in my own sight . . .   2 Samuel 6:21, 22

Here, yet again, there's a glimpse of the world-spirit's offense when the worship of the Most High God does not suit its cultural tastes or calculated reserve. There is a great deal of truth for us to distill as men who today would answer God's call to worship; drawn to answer it in the conviction that to do so is to see more than praise offered to God, but to see spiritual breakthrough unto fruitful witness and the overthrow of dark powers.

If we, like David, will commit to being men of powerful worship, we can be certain we'll be going against the grain of a cynical world. But such humility resisting the "grain" is destined to make a *gain*! The tragic consequences of a soul resistant to that order of humility which governed David's worship of the Lord, is seen in Michal, who despised her husband for openly praising the Lord. The Bible records the sad consequences of her embittered, socially sophisticated mockery: Barrenness.

Unfruitfulness.

Unproductivity.

Unfulfillment.

For Michal's part, from the moment her wrath burned at the sight of her husband's open worship until she eventually laid in her grave, she had no children—the direct result of her unrepentant hatred of her husband's worship.

There's a message, brother. If I resist worship, I restrict life.

And while being cautious to avoid that attitude, I need to be equally cautious to not feel critical or impatient with anyone who, like Michal, opposes worship. If we're honest, we'll probably find that we have at least a tinge of the same tendency buried somewhere in our own hearts. Or at least the potential for such failure.

Case in point: The "Michal" I found seeking a place in my heart.

"Dance for Me"

I have grown unable to read that story without thinking about our human preoccupation with dignity, and being reminded of a brutal confrontation when God brought me to deal with this problem in my own heart. Let me relate the story as recorded in my book, *Worship His Majesty:*

One is hard put at times to know the best way to tell of personal encounters with the Lord. To many people, the mere suggestion of someone's saying, "The Lord spoke to me," is roughly equivalent to claiming they had tea that afternoon on the Planet Venus with alien beings. To others, opinions about the relative validity of your report vary— from the notion you concocted the conversation yourself, to the cautious venturing of the possibility that God just *might* have spoken.

To whatever category my testimony may relegate me in your judgment, I cannot describe one of my most important experiences in Christ without telling you it began with a specific set of words from Him. There were actually only three words—following which neither the Lord nor I spoke. I did argue, debating mentally in my best forensic style as I recoiled from what He had spoken. But each argument was instantly deflated by so irrefutable a rebuttal that my debate was silenced. It hadn't been He who returned my argument. Simple honesty had me cornered. I simply and intuitively knew that to remain honest with God's dealings in my own heart, I had to obey the command of that quiet internal Voice I recognized so well.

"Dance for Me," the Voice said.

That's right. God told me to dance.

I had been at prayer for an extended period of time one morning, using the church sanctuary as my prayer room. No one was there, except for a few staff people in several of the offices. Thus, you can possibly appreciate my dilemma. Even if I did respond to the Voice and perform some holy jig (after all, who can say "No" to God!), what were the chances it would remain between Him and me? What I felt I certainly *didn't* need was for someone to step in and witness the pastor cavorting about like a rank fanatic!

All the thoughts racing through my mind are difficult to summarize, as I futilely attempted to negotiate the situation with the Most High. I could instantly think of innumerable reasons for *not* dancing: it was *impractical, unnecessary, undesirable* and entirely *unreasonable!* And yet none of the reasons was convincing, because deep down I knew the *real* issue. What God was dealing with was not dancing, but dignity, *false* dignity. Raw, carnal, fear-filled, self-centered *pride*.

I was the victim of Michal's Syndrome— that not-so-rare affliction that characterizes those of us who are more preoccupied with our style, sophistication or dignity than we are with being childlike in praising God. Michal's Syndrome is subject to a wide variety of "expert" opinions. Like competing physicians trying to be first to identify a new virus, there are religious analysts who hasten to advance their varied opinions lest a contagion of simplicity rampage through the Church. Their opinions span the spectrum of tastes so much so that if you simply, frankly, flatly *don't* want expressive worship, you can always find a spiritual expert whose "second opinion" will justify yours:

- "Well, some people just *need* a lot of exuberance. Others of us don't." (The implication is that *mature* people don't.)
- "It's all a matter of a person's cultural background. You and I are culturally reserved." (The implication is that "reserved" is socially superior or culturally advanced.)
- "You must watch out for emotionalism; it becomes *so* subjective and worship loses its objectivity in worshiping God and starts to center on man." (The theological concern for "God's glory" obviously makes this righteously unchallengeable.)
- "I believe—don't you?—that everyone should worship God in his own way, and according to his own beliefs. After all, to do otherwise is. . .well, it's. . .it's un-civil." (You know, each of us should worship God according to the dictates of his own heart.)

•	(Smiling smugly) "I wouldn't let it worry me. After all, what difference can it make? God looks on the heart, anyway. All this activity doesn't add a thing!" (The ease with which the leader/counselor/observer dismisses it all as irrelevant consoles our quest for an escape from accountability as to our own responsiveness.)

The issue is expressiveness: openness, forthrightness—any assertive display of praise in worship settings beyond socially acceptable, cooperative singing. It begets a bevy of opinions from wild support to angered resistance. It has made me nervous many times, too.

Several of the above arguments had registered with me over the years, and I could think of the others and more. Having had a broad mixture of church background, running the gamut from Presbyterianism and Methodistism to Pentecostalism, I knew the "do's" and "don'ts" of every circle in evangelical Christianity. When it came to acceptable and unacceptable worship practices, I knew dancing wasn't one that *any* of them smiled on. So I didn't like the idea at *all*, and felt that God Himself was bullying me to the wall on an issue we all had the right to differ over.

I had my theology to stand upon, too.

After all, I knew as I stood there—"Dance for Me" still reverberating through my brain—that God's acceptance of me wasn't based on my antics at praise. I knew He

didn't measure anyone by a set of calisthenics! But just as all these thoughts ran
through my mind, I became aware of one
stark fact: I could win this argument with
myself, but I would risk losing something
with God. I recognized that my potential
"loss" was a hard lesson in humility—

> in remaining as a child before the Father;
> in keeping small in my own eyes;
> in refusing the encrustation of religious
>   sophistry which can inevitably cal-
>   cify the bones of anyone's soul and
>   grip them with a spiritual arthritis.

So, I danced.

I didn't do it well; but then, only God was
looking. And within my heart I felt the
warm, contented witness that Abba Father
was pleased.

I knew His pleasure wasn't because He
had won an argument, but because I had
won a victory. I knew He wasn't happy
because He had managed to exploit my
vulnerability, but because I had chosen to
remain vulnerable. I knew He wasn't dan-
gling me as a pawnlike toy because He
needed my dancing, but because I needed to
respond that way. He knew it was essential
to insure my future flexibility, my availabil-
ity for learning the pathway of worship-
unto-fruitfulness. The last point is so
important—*fruitfulness*. Because the Michal
Syndrome can lead anyone to a rationalized
sense of superiority, it can come at the
expense of a deadly, spiritual fruitlessness.

Barrenness is a high price to pay for one's dignity.*

The Michal Mentality. It's how the world feels about worship, hence, the confrontive nature of worship. Thus, each man will likely face a struggle within himself when the Holy Spirit beckons him to become a committed man of worship.

Brother, it's not an issue of your or my being received or loved any more by our Heavenly Father if we worship according to biblical patterns. The issue at hand isn't our relationship with Him, it's the opening of the doors to new dimensions of kingship—of rulership through the power of the Holy Spirit at work in the broken vessel of a man willing to be humble before His God.

And more. It's an issue of our full recognition and response to such great matters as:

- God's worthiness to be praised;
- His Word's directives for worship; and consequently,
- Our allowing God's Spirit to lead us into deeper expressions of adoration.

And so, Sir, God calls you and me to become men of worship, to do so whole-heartedly not mechanically, responsively not reticently, physically but not fanatically, dynamically but not foolishly.

---

* *Worship His Majesty*, Word Books, pages 127-129. Used by permission.

Such Is the Worship

Foremost in our thinking, let us remember that God is not looking for a parade of noise-makers exercising a set of calisthenics for their own sake. Jesus said, "The Father is seeking those who will worship Him in spirit and in truth." The spirit to which He refers is not only that of a man born again through His Blood, but that begotten in a man who has welcomed the fullness of His Holy Spirit. And the "truth" to which He refers is not only that worship which is settled in Him—The Truth, but which is forthrightly aligned with all the biblical patterns of worship which show how, throughout history, true worshipers have timelessly worshiped the true and living God.

• Such is the worship that the world resists with a vengeance. But God rewards our obedience with supernatural boldness. The Lord says to us as He did to Jeremiah:

"Do not be afraid of their faces, for I am with you to deliver you," says the Lord.
                    Jeremiah 1:8

• Such is the worship which causes hell to tremble in fear, for it is the power of their undoing.

Now when they began to sing and to praise, the Lord set ambushes against the people of Ammon, Moab, and Mount Seir, who had come against Judah; and they were defeated.

2 *Chronicles 20:22*

That's victorious worship, my brother.
Let's go for it!
Together.

**TALK ABOUT IT! Chapter questions
to discuss with a friend.**

1. How do you feel about "dancing
before the Lord"? Have you ever tried it in
your personal worship times—not just when
the worship leader tells you to? Confess
any difficulties with this to another brother,
and invite the Holy Spirit to work a David-
like worship experience in your own life.

2. Pause a moment to take a spiritual
inventory. How did you act at the last
sports event you attended? How does this
compare with your stance in worship?
Discuss ways you can display more zeal in
your personal prayer and praise times
(without being fanatical!).

3. Do you know any other Christians
where you work? Partner with someone to
pray for your company and your co-work-
ers. Ask the Lord to develop Daniel-like
boldness in prayer concerning your work-
place.

Chapter Four
The Invasion of Worship

Invasion: A Weapon of War

For the weapons of our warfare are not carnal but mighty in God for pulling down strongholds, casting down arguments and every high thing that exalts itself against the knowledge of God, bringing every thought into captivity to the obedience of Christ.

2 Corinthians 10:4-5

A hymnal and a rifle.

A worshiping choir and a fighting company of Marines.

A majestic cathedral organ and a Patriot Missile.

. . . Each of these may seem like dichotomous pairs with unrelated partners. At first glance, worship and warfare don't seem to have anything in common except the letter "w". But worship *is* a spiritual weapon.

Consider with me, Sir, the possibility of a man's intertwining worship and warfare. In this passage from Isaiah, observe the relationship between violent spiritual conquest and praise-filled music:

You shall have a song as in the night when a holy festival is kept, and gladness of heart as when one goes with a flute, to come into the mountain of the Lord, to the Mighty One of Israel. The

Lord will cause His glorious voice to be heard, and show the descent of His arm, with the indignation of His anger and the flame of a devouring fire, with scattering, tempest, and hailstones. For through the voice of the Lord, Assyria will be beaten down, who struck with a rod. And in every place where the staff of punishment passes, which the Lord lays on him, it will be with tambourines and harps; and in battles of brandishing He will fight with it.   *Isaiah 30:29-32*

Isaiah gives us a behind-the-scenes look into the spiritual realm wherein God fights enemy hosts with the accompaniment of musical praise and worship from His people—but look at yet another episode. Perhaps the most dramatic biblical account of the warfare aspect of worship is seen when King Jehoshaphat led his people to military victory by putting the choir in front of the army!

And they rose early in the morning and went out into the Wilderness of Tekoa; and as they went out, Jehoshaphat stood and said, "Hear me, O Judah and you inhabitants of Jerusalem: Believe in the Lord your God, and you shall be established; believe His prophets, and you shall prosper." And when he had consulted with the people, he appointed those who should sing to

the Lord, and who should praise the
beauty of holiness, as they went out
before the army and were saying:
"Praise the Lord, for His mercy endures
forever."
                    2 Chronicles 20:20, 21

The enemy was destroyed as the worshipers went first into battle.

Invading the Promised Land

Worship is highly significant to any form
of spiritual battle and it played a key role in
God's people taking possession of the Promised Land. Remember, Israel's preparation
in the wilderness—readying to enter the
Promised Land—was twofold. First, they
received the Law; second, they were in-
structed to build the Tabernacle. It's significant to see how receiving the Word of the
Commandments took about 40 days, but
the preparation of the Tabernacle, and their
learning God's way to worship there, took
about a year. As men, we might well ask
ourselves, "Is it easier for me to listen to and
intellectually assimilate the Bible than it is
to spiritually and practically commit myself
to vital expressions of worship?!"

It's an important consideration, because
Israel's victorious invasion of the land re-
quired a people ready to trust in the Presence of God as well as His Promise. Crucial
to the tearing down of enemy strongholds,
gaining military victory, and forging new

paths into a God-given, promised-land destiny was the worship of God via the tabernacle. His Presence, released by worship, spearheaded the invasion into enemy territory.

Invading Darkness: Songs in the Night

What are the potential implications of these insights for you and me as men living on the edge of the 21st Century? The answer is that while times change, the pathways to power do not. Worship is still the way for invading and winning.

Maybe it's not a promised land you see laying before you.

Maybe it's darkness. Inky black hopelessness that presses in to suffocate you. Silently, it speaks. It denies any hope for the future. It seeks to crush the words God has spoken to you in times past. It strains to erase every memory of joy and light you ever knew.

Darkness speaks. And it must be answered.

In song.

As we'll see, the Lord makes clear that worshiping in song—*even* in, *especially* in, dark times—is a believer's "nuclear arsenal" provided by God to obliterate the enemy and his works.

Now by "song" I'm not referring to our parroting the latest "easy listening" pop tune that has a cheerful message. I'm talking about placing the Word of God on

your lips with heart-embraced melody—
maybe from a chorus you remember from
church, or scriptural truth paraphrased in
your own words and melody—that's just as
potent. Don't worry about *sounding* good.
To sing truth with any degree of sincerity
and the motive of lifting up the Lord—*that's*
what detonates the nuclear explosion against
the forces of hell! The Lord wants to teach
men, all of us, the awesome power of song.

Six in the morning, a hidden corner of the
house, nobody listening, face still unshaven;
nevertheless—a gentle song rises simply
from the lips of a man gutsy enough to defy
his own fragile ego which clamors for protec-
tion against change—and fights to keep a
self-perceived dignity intact, a dignity that
loves nothing but itself.

Yes, it cuts. Like circumcision, growing
in worship can cut—but it cuts away fear,
doubt, and pride.

And worship in song also cuts right
through the wall of darkness, shredding,
with hurricane violence, the clouds of black-
ness trying to engulf your tomorrows with
doom. Such worship comes with a price,
but it buys so much more than you can
imagine! God eagerly awaits for the moment
you part your lips in song. For by it, you are
tuning up to the symphony of Heaven, where
the Song is being sung eternally, and by
tuning up to Heaven's frequency, you usher
in the dominion of God whose praises you
sing!

You have nothing to sing about?—only futility, despair, and hopelessness? Then you're the *perfect candidate* to launch forth in song . . . according to the reasoning of the Lord:

*"**Sing, O barren,** you who have not borne! Break forth into singing, and cry aloud, you who have not labored with child! For more are the children of the desolate than the children of the married woman," says the Lord.*

Isaiah 54:1

How Lord? How could you ask us to do the *opposite* of what we feel like doing? Answer: if you do what you *feel* like doing, you'll just continue to despair. Right? When you're despairing, you don't *feel* like rejoicing before God. But how potent a spiritual weapon this is!

*For this cause everyone who is godly shall pray to You in a time when You may be found; surely in a flood of great waters they shall not come near him. You are my hiding place; You shall preserve me from trouble; You shall surround me with **songs of deliverance.** Selah   Psalm 32:6-7*

Why in the world would singing result in our deliverance? Because the oppressive works of hell cannot tolerate the singing of saints who refuse to be overtaken by circumstances and spiritual oppression, but instead lift their voices heavenward in song!

*Let the word of Christ dwell in you richly in all wisdom, teaching and admonishing one another in psalms and hymns and **spiritual songs**, singing with grace in your hearts to the Lord.*

Colossians 3:16

*And do not be drunk with wine, in which is dissipation; but be filled with the Spirit, speaking to one another in psalms and hymns and **spiritual songs**, singing and making melody in your heart to the Lord.*

Ephesians 5:18-19

The above words from two of Paul's letters merge together to teach us the power of song to (1) keep you filled with the Holy Spirit, and (2) make the Word of God alive and powerful in your spirit and soul. It almost seems that worshiping in song provides the spiritual enzymes by which the "meat of the Word" is digested and assimilated into our lives.

*Where were you when I laid the foundations of the earth? Tell Me, if you have understanding. Who determined its measurements? Surely you know! Or who stretched the line upon it? To what were its foundations fastened? Or who laid its cornerstone, when **the morning stars sang together,** and all the sons of God shouted for joy?*

Job 38:4-7

In this passage, God describes to Job a behind-the-scenes view of creation when

God's majestic art and wisdom hurled the universe into existence amid angelic song.

Think with me a moment about that. Creation. Accompanied by song. Could there be a connection? Of course there was at the time of Creation eons ago, but what about *now*? Could there be a universal spiritual dynamic still in force today?

I believe the Lord would have us understand that if we would enter into worshipful song more freely, more often, it would release Him to work far more creatively in life's circumstances. And whatever blessing or goodness the Lord wants to work in our lives—even if it doesn't exist yet—He can create it. Out of nothing . . . nothing but your song.

Paul knows what he's talking about when he says, "I will sing with the spirit, and I will also sing with the understanding" (1 Cor. 14:15b). His dramatic first-hand experience with the power of song is recorded in Acts 16:25-34. When he sang in worship, the bondage of a Philippian dungeon was shattered; and as a result, salvation came to the jailer's household.

Paul's song broke chains and flung open prison doors. The same power of song waits to be born on your lips, too.

Not long ago, in one of our men's meetings, hundreds of men were praising God with a holy boldness. It was a glorious time. At the conclusion of this "high worship" time, the Holy Spirit spoke through a word of prophecy. He said: "Against many of you the enemy of your souls has suppressed the childlike freedom to sing. He has kept you from singing ever since your adolescence when your voices changed. You felt embarrassed at the awkward irregularity of your voice. It sounded neither like a man nor a boy, but rather hovered in a transitional 'no man's land' of indecisiveness. Therefore, many of you no longer sing." But God declared that evening, "I'm bringing you to have a man's voice—a voice of authority and freedom to sing. For you have seen how a clear, powerful voice can literally shatter glass. And so there are obstacles that the Adversary has put before you in your life. But if you use your voice of worship—moving into boldness, confidence, and clarity of focus on Me—I will shatter, with your voice of praise, those barriers in your life that have seemed so impenetrable! So praise Me, My sons, worship with a bold, new voice!"

Let's pick up the theme, brother!

Sing!! And watch God break through in creative power and with shattering deliverance from bondage.

TALK ABOUT IT! Chapter questions to discuss with a friend.

1. Consider how you might wage spiritual warfare through praise and worship, followed by intercessory prayer, for a situation you're facing in your life right now. Share your prayer burden with another brother and plan your battle strategy.

2. Is it easier for you to play "Bible Trivia"—intellectually assimilating biblical teachings—than to spiritually and practically commit yourself to expressions of worship? If so, confess your tendency to trust in your own understanding instead of leaning on Him (Prov. 3:5, 6) and begin to open up to the Holy Spirit's leading in this vital area.

3. Do you make a regular practice of "singing in the spirit"? Pray together with another brother about any perceived inadequacies you feel about your voice and receive the promise of the word of prophecy written above. Practice singing bold praises to the Lord: in your car, in the shower, wherever you can!

Chapter Five
Worship:
Key to Evangelism

It was like being hit in the head with a five-pound sledge hammer!

Seated in the 8,000-seat convention center, I was listening to a man present *The First Ministry of Evangelism* to the massive group of pastors with whom I was seated in the giant arena. The thing he just said had stunned me: "The foundational pathway to evangelism is the cultivation of a people who will worship God."

I'd never heard anything like that.

Everything in my thoroughly evangelical background had been rooted in methods, training programs, witnessing campaigns, soul-winning approaches, altar workers guidelines, crusades and outreaches, etc. But worship?

Well, I believed in worship all right. And I knew that it wasn't unimportant. But it did seem like something remote to evangelism. To my mind "worship" was something Christians did *after* they were saved, *not* something they did in order to *see* people saved. I was puzzled by the speaker's proposition.

He went on: "Look at Acts 13," he exclaimed. And turning there, my attention was drawn to one of the most pivotal places and times in the history of the Early Church.

The place: Antioch, the new center of revival, where the Holy Spirit was moving in power.

The time: A season of waiting on the Lord for His purposes in the midst of this revival blessing.

I sat forward in my seat, looking around at the other 8,000 in the room, to see if they were feeling the awakening that was occurring in my soul. The speaker continued:

"Notice that 'as they ministered to the Lord and fasted,' the Word says that the Holy Spirit began to speak and to direct activities which became the most historic strategy for global evangelism since Jesus gave the great commission."

I knew what he was talking about. It's right after this time of "ministry to the Lord" (which is a biblical expression for worshiping) that Paul and Barnabas set forth on their first world-shaking missionary journey. I was starting to see it: *WORSHIP PRECEDES EVANGELISM*. The case was expanded from earlier events as I began to capture the principle:

• At Pentecost, the outpouring of the Holy Spirit produced supernatural *worship*: "We hear them speaking in our own tongues the wonderful works of God" (Acts 2:11). While Peter's preaching brought 3,000 decisions, it was praise and worship which drew the crowd and impressed the

76

onlookers that they were seeing a miracle manifestation of God's Presence.

• I suddenly saw also how God had delivered Israel from Egypt to bring His nation to be (1) a people of blessed purpose (Ex. 3:15-17), and (2) a witness to the nations (Ex. 19:6). BUT . . . but the *key* to this realization would be *worship*, and the *pathway* to their purpose and victory would be via Sinai's Law (God's Word) and Moses' Tabernacle (God's worship). The fruit of their learning to know and honor God in worship resulted eventually in a people who conquered the land of God's purposed possession for them.

So there it was: Worship paves the way to evangelism! Worship is the pathway to expanded boundaries! I could see it in the Word, though I never had before, and it immediately began to change my life.

The result was to introduce the small group of people at the new pastorate I accepted shortly thereafter, to a priority of *"ministering to the Lord."* Taking that phrase from the Acts 13 record, and noting its repetition in the OT record of the priestly ministry of Aaron and his sons (Ex. 28:41; 29:1, 44; 30:30; et. al.) we committed to become a people of worship. These basic guidelines governed this pursuit:

• We would not apologize for biblical expressions of worship, but we would consistently explain them with graciousness, in a way that would invite but not coerce participation. *Discovery: People wanted to be free to worship expressively, and did—but for a reason.* The reason—

• We refused to be either mystical, unseemly, or fanatical in our expressiveness. In other words, we contended that spiritual worship would also logically be as sensitive, sensible, and scriptural as it was open, free, and joyous. *Discovery: Biblical controls prohibited foolishness, and spiritual sensitivity brought unity and a choir-like joining together in a loving worship of the Lord.*

Of course, expressiveness was the challenge. Most church worship forms don't present any problem (other than a possibility for deadness, dryness, or flesh-pampering caution) unless they are openly expressed. But by pursuing a biblical child-likeness, a joyous, gentle freedom filled the house whenever we came together.

But there was one key to it all which I've rarely mentioned.

Men who worship.

That is, cultivating men who would become *active* in worship.

I learned early on that if the men don't move into worship leadership, a certain kind of tinniness and short-lived exuberance was the best we could manage. If the body was to rise as a worshiping assembly, the men of the congregation would need to lead the way.

Not necessarily as singers.

Not necessarily as musicians.

Not necessarily as public leaders.

But the release of worship awaited a cadre of committed men who would lay aside male reserve and whatever vestige of pride would seek to find a haven in some secret corner of our souls—and worship!

Worship with full-bodied singing.

Worship with a ready understanding.

Worship with forthright joyousness.

Worship with "holy hands" upraised.

Worship and magnify the Savior as disciples who have answered His call to "Follow Me," and to follow Him right into the presence of the Father with praiseful song and biblically directed, soul-humbling, life-transforming worship.

The result was as had been predicted by the teacher who touched my heart with that transforming viewpoint—*Worship First*!

Evangelism followed. Marvelously, mightily, and continually.

As of the date of this writing, it is difficult to enumerate the whole of the record of God's grace in evangelistic results where worship was put in its biblical place—FIRST, and with MEN leading the way.

In the nearly 25 years since beginning, more than 40,000 decisions for Jesus Christ have been realized at our church services. More than 30 churches have been planted elsewhere, and over 100 pastors and church leaders have gone out from this one congregation to serve the Body of Christ. More than 100 nations are touched in some way each year by evangelistic enterprises reaching out from this worship center, and more than $20 million have been given away to serve human need and the spread of the Gospel of the Kingdom of God from Los Angeles to the far corners of the earth.

The Central Focus

But the central focus in this writing is to you, my brother. To you as a man who—like Abraham, Moses, David, Daniel, Peter, and Paul—God has called to worship Him "in spirit and in truth."

I have concluded with a testimony of God's dealing with me—one man. And the impact affected a whole "house"—the family of an entire congregation which grew and continues to do so as we worship the Lord today. But I began another way.

I began by sharing the story of another man named Jack. A roofing contractor who had a tough situation to deal with in his family, and who recognized that his role as a worshiping man might hold the key to the dominion of God's Kingdom over the situation. And it did. He worshiped God. God won the victory. Jack rejoiced in the aftermath. Hallelujah!

And so the "Hallelujahs!" are waiting to roll—

In heaven, as we join the angel hosts in praise-filled worship;
On earth, as we take our place

80

shoulder-to-shoulder as men at worship in our gatherings;

In the invisible, as hell's powers are put to flight by our praises to the Most High; and

In our homes and communities, where transformed possibilities are truly present if worshiping men can be found.

The man who worships has already begun his witness. But the man who worships will find his presence and his words become welcomed by the needy and hungry among whom he lives and with whom he works. While the world may at times mock the worshiping man, when that same society's systems crumble, when the sick suffer, when the homes collapse, when the problems are pressing on people you meet—it's to the worshiping man the world turns.

And that's when the testimony of Jesus the Savior is yours and mine to give. Our witness of His power to save will find ready entrance among those who have been watching a man like you.

A man of true worship, before the true and living God.

TALK ABOUT IT! Chapter questions to discuss with a friend.

1. Take a moment to partner in prayer with a brother about your unsaved friends and family members. Begin with worship and thanksgiving, and ask the Lord to release pathways into their hearts and lives through the witness of your worshipful lifestyle.

2. Why is it important for men to move into worship leadership? Describe any reticence you may feel about your own participation in leading in worship and discuss ways you see how this temptation to timidity can be overcome.

3. You don't need to be on the church platform in order to be a worship leader: You can take more initiative when praying with friends or you can boldly lift your voice in praise during corporate worship and be an example to those around you in the congregation. Choose to be a worship leader in your arena of influence, whatever it may be!

DEVOTIONS
FROM SELECTED
PSALMS

Contributed by Bob Anderson

The Book of Psalms, written over a significant span of time from 1000—300 B.C., was authored by several men including King David, Solomon, Moses, Asaph, the Sons of Korah, and others. It contains a collection of hymns and prayers used for worship in Solomon's Temple as well as additional songs which were incorporated into the psalter later on.

The Psalms are rich in Hebrew poetry, a writing style primarily distinguished by the rhyming of thoughts instead of words.

It's interesting to note that about half of the references to the Messiah recorded by New Testament writers come directly from the Book of Psalms. Even Jesus confirms the Messianic prophecy of the Psalms in Luke 24:44.

The outstanding themes throughout this book are *prayer* and *praise* to the Most High God. The worship it instructs exceeds quiet devotional thoughts, encouraging active expressions of worship such as: clapping and shouting (47:1), bowing (95:6), lifting up of hands (141:2), and dancing (149:3).

(It is suggested that this devotional be used for stimulating discussion and prayer within a small group of men meeting regularly.)

□ **Today's Text: Psalm 1** *(key vv. 2-3)*

1 **Today's Truth:** The Hebrew word for "meditate" transcends the idea of silent reflection upon the Word of God meaning "to mutter or make a quiet sound upon one's lips." That's the picture of a person *totally* immersed in God's Word! The promised results: prosperity in every area of life and upon all that we do!

Today's Thoughts:——————————

—————————————————————

—————————————————————

□ **Today's Text: Psalm 4** *(key v. 7)*

2 **Today's Truth:** God gives us the power to enjoy what we have and to be glad in any situation—*more* than those people who have riches and good fortune but don't serve the Lord (Ecc. 5:10,19). Without God, life's blessings are meaningless and powerless to fill us with joy.

Today's Thoughts: ———————————

—————————————————————

—————————————————————

□ **Today's Text: Psalm 8** *(key v.3)*

3 **Today's Truth:** David extols the One who constructed the Universe with His *fingers*. Certainly our personal problems can be borne by the *hands* of God whose mere *fingerwork* spans the greatest distances measured by man—more than 100 million light years of awesome craftsmanship!

Today's Thoughts: ———————————

—————————————————————

—————————————————————

☐ **Today's Text: Psalm 18** *(key vv. 11-14)*

4 **Today's Truth:** When we walk through the "valley of the shadow of death" or struggle through a season of personal darkness—not able to see "where God is" or what He is doing—we can rest in the knowledge that our darkness is God's hiding place. He is in there *with us* even though we can't see Him. And at the right moment, God will "thunder from heaven" and fight for us!

Today's Thoughts: _____

_____

_____

☐ **Today's Text: Psalm 20** *(key v. 7)*

5 **Today's Truth:** Some people trust in physical power to deliver them, but we have the Name of the Lord—a resource of help *far more solid* than earth's physical foundations. Though even the best of us may be tempted to look to the world for help when trials burn hot, time proves over and over that the Creator of everything is our security.

Today's Thoughts: _____

_____

_____

☐ **Today's Text: Psalm 22** *(key v. 1)*

6 **Today's Truth:** This psalm is rich in Messianic prophecy accurately predicting events in Jesus' life 1000 years before they happened! Only God could have fulfilled such prophetic complexity!

Today's Thoughts: _____

_____

_____

☐ **Today's Text: Psalm 23** *(key v. 6)*

7 **Today's Truth:** The scope of this psalm is precious and all-encompassing. <u>In this life</u>, goodness and mercy *shall pursue us!* . . . and throughout <u>all eternity</u> we'll *dwell with God* in His house! . . . if we'll only follow the Great Shepherd.

Today's Thoughts: ————————

————————————————————

————————————————————

☐ **Today's Text: Psalm 25** *(key v. 1)*

8 **Today's Truth:** Sometimes the *gravity* of our trials or the *depth* of our pain occasions a *simple* posture: lifting up our souls to God. It's like a child lifting up a badly cut finger, "Owiee! Fix it, Daddy! Make it better!"

Today's Thoughts: ————————

————————————————————

————————————————————

☐ **Today's Text: Psalm 32** *(key v. 1)*

9 **Today's Truth:** The condition of a person whose sins have been forgiven is "blessed," which literally means: "happy!" No one needs to be lost—no matter how vile his sins—if only he'll accept Jesus. God made salvation so simple that a child can understand and enter in, and yet so compelling that a scholar, if willing to come with simple faith as a child, can know the Lord.

Today's Thoughts: ————————

————————————————————

————————————————————

☐ **Today's Text: Psalm 34** *(key v. 19)*

10 Today's Truth: Good! Just because I'm having an abundance of tough times, doesn't mean God is angry with me! Righteous people experience many afflictions, the Word says. 1 Pet. 5:9 encourages us that we're not alone in our sufferings. But we remain confident because of the promise: *God delivers the righteous out of them all!*

Today's Thoughts: _____

_____

_____

☐ **Today's Text: Psalm 45** *(key v. 1)*

11 Today's Truth: Our tongues should be like the pen of a ready writer—poised to lift up articulate praise to God. Here the psalmist uses his imagination to extol the Lord in fresh, powerful ways. What a talent to cultivate: finding *new ways* to tell the Lord how great He is!

Today's Thoughts: _____

_____

_____

☐ **Today's Text: Psalm 47** *(key v. 1)*

12 Today's Truth: For some of us, open and strong praise is difficult either because we were raised to be ''quietly reverent'' or because we feel that bold worship might turn us into fanatics. But should our cheers for our favorite sports team outdo our enthusiasm towards the Almighty? Selah.

Today's Thoughts: _____

_____

_____

☐ **Today's Text: Psalm 51** *(key v. 10)*

13 Today's Truth: David's heart-rending psalm of repentance has at its center the plea for a clean heart and a steadfast spirit. Forgiveness was not enough—David wanted strength to avoid future sin. But he knew he needed a redeemed nature from God's Spirit in order to continue to be victorious in the face of future temptation.

Today's Thoughts: _____

_____

_____

☐ **Today's Text: Psalm 55** *(key v. 22)*

14 Today's Truth: Reminiscent of 1 Peter 5:7, this verse affirms that if we cast our cares on God, He will sustain us. *Sustain* is a "power" word, meaning: to support, protect, provide food, nourish, defend, and give all means needed for living.

Today's Thoughts: _____

_____

_____

☐ **Today's Text: Psalm 62** *(key v. 11)*

15 Today's Truth: The human mind boggles. It isn't that "lots of power" belongs to God. Rather, *POWER* belongs to God. Period. When we worship Jesus, we are in touch with ALL POWER . . . available to flow into any of life's situations!

Today's Thoughts: _____

_____

_____

☐ **Today's Text: Psalm 63** *(key v. 1)*

16 **Today's Truth:** David set himself to seek God *early*. With pressurized schedules the way they are nowadays, often the only time left to carve from is the tail end of sleep! But the sacrifice of early worship is rewarded by God's rulership throughout the day. For God is "enthroned in the praises of His people" (Ps. 22:3).

Today's Thoughts: _____

_____

_____

☐ **Today's Text: Psalm 71** *(key vv. 20-21)*

17 **Today's Truth:** Although God allows troubles in our lives, He is quick and desirious to lift us out of our "pit" of despair, "bundle us up" in comfort, and enlarge the dimensions of our destinies!

Today's Thoughts: _____

_____

_____

☐ **Today's Text: Psalm 91** *(key vv. 11-12)*

18 **Today's Truth:** The Lord has given His angels as guardians over us. Apparently, *more* than one angel has been personally assigned to each of us as evidenced by the plural text. In heaven we may discover the myriad of ways they protected us!

Today's Thoughts: _____

_____

_____

☐ **Today's Text: Psalm 100** *(key v. 4)*

19 **Today's Truth:** This verse indicates that it's always good to approach the Lord with thanksgiving and praise on our lips—as opposed to popping into His presence with prayer requests and leaving just as quickly, devoid of any worship or gratitude.

Today's Thoughts: _____

_____

_____

☐ **Today's Text: Psalm 103** *(key v. 2)*

20 **Today's Truth:** David commands his own soul not to forget all of God's benefits, and then he proceeds to enumerate scores of them. At times when we are most downcast, it is all the more critical to speak aloud all that God has done for us throughout our lives.

Today's Thoughts: _____

_____

_____

☐ **Today's Text: Psalm 107** *(key v. 31)*

21 **Today's Truth:** The psalmist almost groans while expressing his wish for men to give thanks to God. Obviously, God's unceasing work throughout the world far outnumbers the people who thank Him.

Today's Thoughts: _____

_____

_____

☐ **Today's Text: Psalm 112** *(key vv. 1-3)*

22 Today's Truth: With such promises of God's spectacular and all-encompassing blessing upon those who diligently cleave to Him, it's amazing we don't worship Him more freely, more diligently, more often. People who do will find their hearts transformed by the nearness of His presence. Such are the people in whom God can trust with prosperity—because of the selfless love that's born in their hearts through praise.

Today's Thoughts: _____

_____

_____

☐ **Today's Text: Psalm 121** *(key vv. 7-8)*

23 Today's Truth: God's preservation of our souls from all evil during "our going out and coming in" is predicated on our eyes being lifted to Him in confident faith that He—Maker of Heaven and Earth—is our only true help.

Today's Thoughts: _____

_____

_____

☐ **Today's Text: Psalm 122** *(key v. 1)*

24 Today's Truth: David loved worshiping the Lord so much, the mere mention of going to the house of the Lord brought joy!

Today's Thoughts: _____

_____

_____

☐ **Today's Text: Psalm 126** *(key v. 1)*

25 **Today's Truth:** When the Lord brings full redemption and freedom to His saints, it can almost seem like a wonderful dream—too good to be true. But that's God's goal for us: abundant life, wherein He causes us to inherit beauty for ashes, and wherein He makes our former darkness to shine as the noonday sun (Isaiah 58:10; 61:3).

Today's Thoughts: _____

_____

_____

☐ **Today's Text: Psalm 127** *(key v. 1)*

26 **Today's Truth:** Our best effort without the Lord's blessing is an exercise in *futility*. Our expecting God to do everything without our obedient participation is *presumption*. This verse speaks of balance between human endeavor and Omnipotent *involvement*.

Today's Thoughts: _____

_____

_____

 Today's Text: Psalm 139 *(key vv. 23-24)*

27 **Today's Truth:** David's quickness to seek the Lord's righteousness and lay his heart bare before Him helped cause him to be known as "a man after God's own heart" (1 Sam. 13:14).

Today's Thoughts: _____

_____

_____

☐ **Today's Text: Psalm 141** *(key v. 2)*

28 **Today's Truth:** What personal sacrifices do we make by raising our hands in worship to God?—Fleshly pride. Independence. Arrogance. False dignity. And what beautiful things does such a sacrifice of worship work within us? Humility. Grace. Power. A child-like spirit.

Today's Thoughts: _____

_____

_____

☐ **Today's Text: Psalm 145** *(key v. 4)*

29 **Today's Truth:** It is critical for us parents to instill within our kids a vital, personal faith—one in which they have a vested ownership. As the Book of Judges shows us, God's blessing and revelation can be lost in just one quick generation.

Today's Thoughts: _____

_____

_____

☐ **Today's Text: Psalm 149** *(key v. 3)*

30 **Today's Truth:** For most of us, the idea of dancing before the Lord induces embarrassment. Who among us can dance with skill, confidence, or precision? Very few. Yet a praiseful swaying of upraised hands with a simple step of the feet in worship—and in God's eyes—you're beyond Baryshnikov!

Today's Thoughts: _____

_____

_____

☐ **Today's Text: Psalm 150** *(key v. 6)*

31 **Today's Truth:** A fitting conclusion to the psalter is this repetitive exhortation to let all who have breath "praise Him, praise Him, praise Him . . . " (ad infinitum, amen, and hallelujah!). In other words, if you are still breathing, worship the Lord!

Today's Thoughts: _____

_____

_____

Additional Resources for Biblical Manhood

Available from Jack Hayford and
Living Way Ministries

AUDIO CASSETTE MINI-ALBUMS (2 tapes)

Honest to God	SC122	$8
Redeeming Relationships for Men & Women	SC177	$8
Why Sex Sins Are Worse Than Others	SC179	$8
How God Uses Men	SC223	$8
A Father's Approval	SC225	$8
Resisting the Devil	SC231	$8
How to Recession-Proof Your Home	SC369	$8
Safe Sex!	SC448	$8
The Leader Jesus Trusts	SC461	$8

AUDIO CASSETTE ALBUMS (# of tapes)

Cleansed for the Master's Use (3)	SC377	$13
Becoming God's Man (4)	SC457	$17
Fixing Family Fractures (4)	SC217	$17
The Power of Blessing (4)	SC395	$17
Men's Seminars 1990-91 (10)	MSEM	$42
Premarital Series (12)	PM02	$50
A Family Encyclopedia (24)	SC233	$99

VHS VIDEO ALBUMS

Why Sex Sins Are Worse Than Others	WSSV	$19
Divorce and the People of God	DIVV	$19
Earthly Search for a Heavenly Father	ESFV	$19

Add 15% for shipping and handling.
California residents add 8.25% sales tax.

Request your free Resource Catalog.

Living Way Ministries Resources
14820 Sherman Way • Van Nuys, CA 91405-2233
(818) 779-8480 or (800) 776-8180